Going Green

When you get home from school do you:

- Turn on the lights?
- Get a drink from the fridge?
- Put a snack in the microwave?
- Turn on the TV?

If you do, you have used lots of power.

Where does power come from?

There are two kinds of power. Some power comes from the sun, the wind and water. This is called renewable power because it is renewed all the time and it never runs out.

POWER PACK

Contents

Haydn Middleton

Story illustrated by
Leo Hartas

Heinemann

Find out about

- How to save power

Tricky words

- fridge
- microwave
- renewable
- fossil fuel
- wasting
- blades
- solar
- museum

Introduce these tricky words and help the reader when they come across them later!

Text starter

There are two kinds of power: renewable power and fossil fuel power. We are running out of fossil fuel, but we can get power from the wind, sun, water and even poo. We need to be more 'green' and to save power.

The other kind of power is called fossil fuel power.

Fossil fuel is made from the fossils of animals and plants that died millions of years ago. The fossils become coal, gas and oil.

Most of our power comes from burning fossil fuel.

Wasting power

Now the bad news ... all over the world people are using too much fossil fuel.

Every time you turn on a light, turn on the TV or travel in a car you are using up fossil fuel. If we are not careful we will run out of it.

Lots of people do not know how much power they are wasting. If you forget to turn off a light, or if you leave the TV on stand-by, you are wasting power. If we always turned off lights we are not using, we would save enough power for more than five hospitals!

Fossil fuel alert

If we run out of fossil fuel, where will our power come from?

Don't panic!

There are things we can do to get power without using fossil fuel – like using renewable power sources.

Wind power

In windy places we can have wind farms.
A wind farm is a group of windmills
with big blades. When the wind spins
the blades, power is made.
We're never going to run out of wind!
But not many places are windy enough
to have wind farms.

The wind must blow at 9mph to turn the blades.

Solar power

In sunny places we can have solar panels. Solar panels are put on roofs. The sun warms the panels and this gives enough power to heat and light a house. People also build cars that are powered by solar panels.

Solar-powered cars race across Australia each year!

Water power

In places where water is moving very fast, we can use the water to make power. This dam can provide enough power for two million homes!

In places where the sea has big waves, we can use the waves to make power.

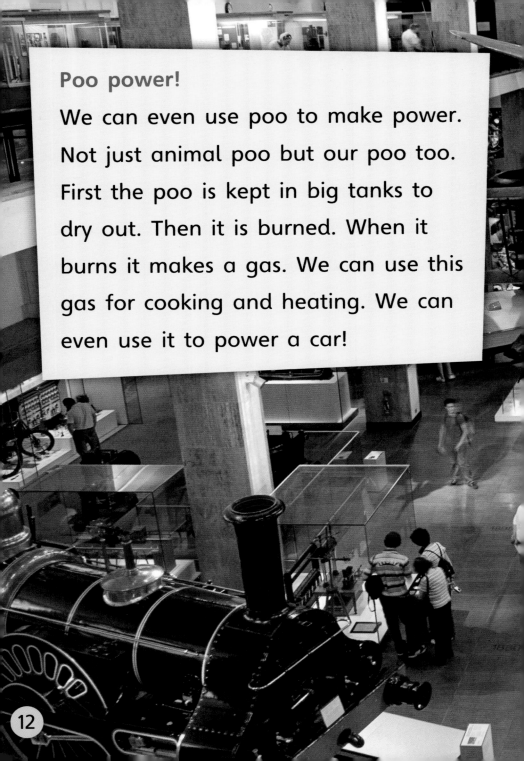

Poo power!

We can even use poo to make power. Not just animal poo but our poo too. First the poo is kept in big tanks to dry out. Then it is burned. When it burns it makes a gas. We can use this gas for cooking and heating. We can even use it to power a car!

The Science Museum in London plans to use the poo from the three million people who visit each year.

The gas from the poo would help to heat and light the museum.

So what can you do to save fossil fuel?

- Wear warm clothes and turn down the heating.
- Don't leave the TV or computer on stand-by.
- Turn off lights when you are not using them.
- Walk or cycle when you can.

Quiz

Text Detective

- Can you name some renewable power sources?
- How would your life change if there was no more fossil fuel?

Word Detective

- **Phonic Focus:** Identifying and spelling word endings
  Page 4: Find two past tense verbs ending with 'ed'.
  What sound does each 'ed' ending make?
  (called, d; renewed, d)
- Page 9: Find a word that means 'turns'.
- Page 14: Why do you think the author used bullet points on this page?

Super Speller

Read these words:

died   build   using

Now try to spell them!

HA! HA! HA!

Q What's green and jumps around the garden?

A A spring onion!

In this story

 Alex

 Sarah

Tricky words

- Internet
- wastes
- blazing
- whispered
- forging
- peered
- siren
- bundled

Introduce these tricky words and help the reader when they come across them later!

Story starter

Alex and Sarah care about the environment. They are members of a green kids' club, and they are always looking for ways to encourage people to 'think green'! One day Alex and Sarah were in the library, using the Internet to find out about ways to save power.

Lights Out at Night!

Alex and Sarah were using the Internet to find out about ways to save power. "Look at this," said Alex. "Leaving on just one light wastes so much power!" "I bet people don't know that," said Sarah.

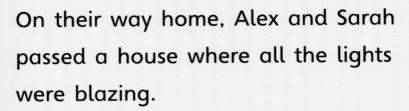

On their way home, Alex and Sarah passed a house where all the lights were blazing.

"Those lights are very bright," said Sarah, "and I saw they were on all day yesterday too."

"They must have forgotten to turn them off," said Alex.

"We should tell them," said Sarah.

"Let's knock on the door."

Alex and Sarah went up the garden path. An empty bin was rolling around and the garden was full of rubbish. "What a mess!" said Sarah.

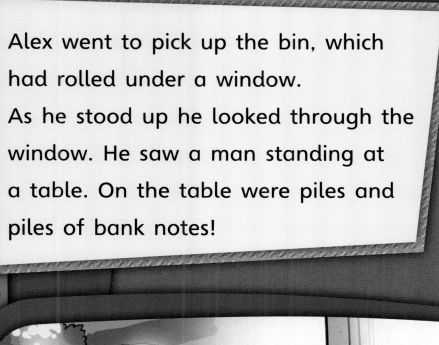

Alex went to pick up the bin, which had rolled under a window.
As he stood up he looked through the window. He saw a man standing at a table. On the table were piles and piles of bank notes!

What do you think the bank notes are for?

Alex and Sarah looked in the window.
"What is he doing?" whispered Sarah.
"I don't know," said Alex.
"Why does he need so many lights?"
asked Sarah.

They watched as the man took a pile of bank notes over to a copier.

"I know what he's doing," said Alex. "He's forging bank notes and they look just like real notes."

"We've got to tell the police," said Sarah, getting out her mobile phone.

But as Sarah turned to make the call she tripped over the rubbish bin. "Ow!" she cried as her phone fell from her hand and landed on the path.

"Sshhh!" whispered Alex, but he was too late. The man looked up and saw Alex at the window.

"What do you think you're doing?" he shouted angrily.

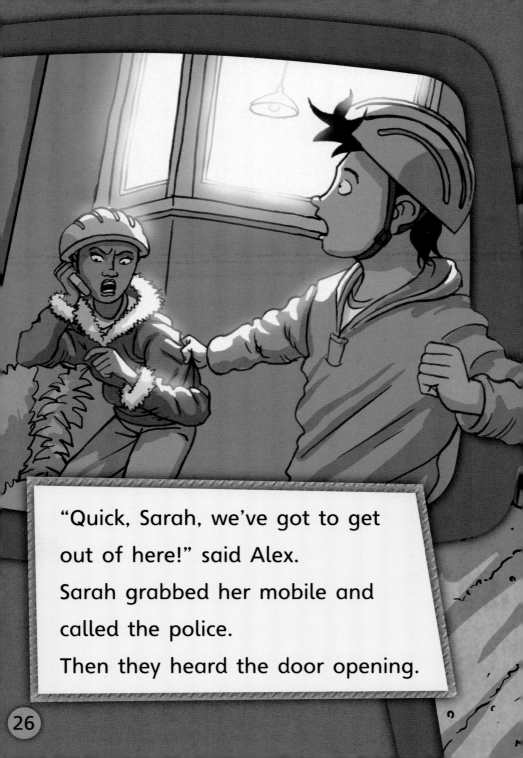

"Quick, Sarah, we've got to get out of here!" said Alex.

Sarah grabbed her mobile and called the police.

Then they heard the door opening.

Looking round, they saw the man standing in the doorway. He was holding a baseball bat.
"Run, Sarah!" shouted Alex, and they ran down the path.

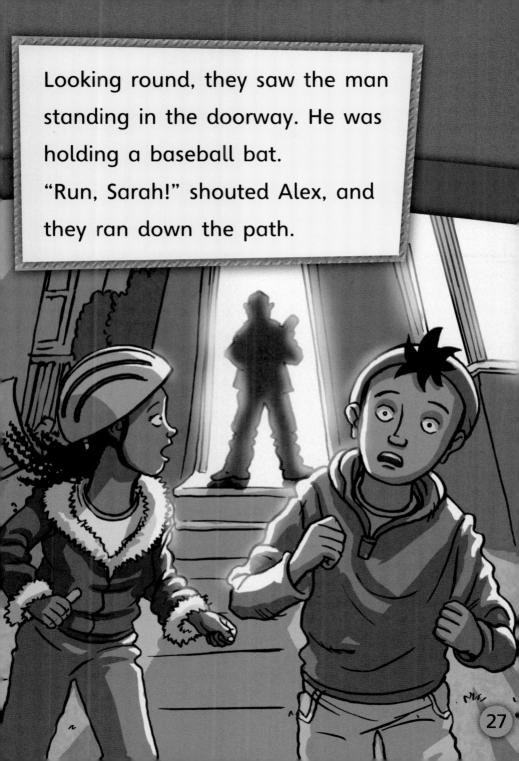

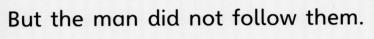

But the man did not follow them.
He went back into the house, slamming
the door behind him.
Alex and Sarah crept back up the path
and peered through the window.

The man was stuffing the piles of
bank notes into a big black bag.
Then he grabbed his car keys.
"He's getting away!" said Sarah.
But just then they saw a blue flashing
light and heard a siren.

Two police officers jumped out of the car
and ran round to the back of the house.
Minutes later they returned.
One police officer was leading the man
by the arm and the other was holding
the big black bag.

"What made you look through the window?" said one of the officers as he bundled the man into the back of the police car.

"We were going to tell him about saving power," said Alex.

"Lucky for us you're so green!" said the police officer.

Quiz

Text Detective

- Why was the man cross when he saw Alex and Sarah?
- What would you do if you discovered someone forging bank notes?

Word Detective

- **Phonic Focus:** Identifying and spelling word endings
  Page 24: Find four past tense verbs ending with 'ed'.
  What sound does each 'ed' ending make?
  (turned, d; tripped, t; cried, d; landed, ed)
- Page 25: Find two different speech verbs.
- Page 28: Find a word that means 'looked'.

Super Speller

Read these words:

leaving yesterday watched

Now try to spell them!

HA! HA! HA!

Q Why did the belt get arrested?

A Because it held up some trousers!